# Data Science for Business

*Predictive Modeling, Data Mining, Data Analytics, Data Warehousing, Data Visualization, Regression Analysis, Database Querying, and Machine Learning for Beginners*

© **Copyright 2018**

All rights Reserved. No part of this book may be reproduced in any form without permission in writing from the author. Reviewers may quote brief passages in reviews.

Disclaimer: No part of this publication may be reproduced or transmitted in any form or by any means, mechanical or electronic, including photocopying or recording, or by any information storage and retrieval system, or transmitted by email without permission in writing from the publisher.

While all attempts have been made to verify the information provided in this publication, neither the author nor the publisher assume any responsibility for errors, omissions or contrary interpretations of the subject matter herein.

Any persons or organizations referred to herein are composites for the purpose of illustration and do not represent real persons or organizations.

This book is for entertainment purposes only. The views expressed are those of the author alone, and should not be taken as expert instruction or commands. The reader is responsible for his or her own actions.

Adherence to all applicable laws and regulations, including international, federal, state and local laws governing professional licensing, business practices, advertising and all other aspects of doing business in the US, Canada, UK or any other jurisdiction is the sole responsibility of the purchaser or reader.

Neither the author nor the publisher assumes any responsibility or liability whatsoever on the behalf of the purchaser or reader of these materials. Any perceived slight of any individual or organization is purely unintentional.

# Contents

INTRODUCTION .................................................................................... 1

CHAPTER 1: WHAT IS DATA SCIENCE? .................................................. 2

CHAPTER 2: HOW BIG DATA WORKS IN DATA SCIENCE ................... 11

CHAPTER 3: EXPLORATIVE DATA ANALYSIS ........................................ 18

CHAPTER 4: WORKING WITH DATA MINING ..................................... 22

CHAPTER 5: DATA MINING TEXT ........................................................ 27

CHAPTER 6: BASIC MACHINE LEARNING ALGORITHMS TO KNOW ................................................................................................... 32

CHAPTER 7: DATA MODELING ............................................................ 42

CHAPTER 8: DATA VISUALIZATION ..................................................... 47

CHAPTER 9: HOW TO USE DATA SCIENCE RIGHT ............................. 52

CHAPTER 10: TIPS FOR DATA SCIENCE .............................................. 55

CHAPTER 11: WORKING ON A DESCRIPTIVE ANALYSIS .................. 62

**CHAPTER 12: WORKING WITH PREDICTIVE ANALYTICS IN DATA SCIENCE** .................................................................................. 67

**CHAPTER 13: WHY DOES MY COMPANY NEED TO WORK WITH PREDICTIVE ANALYTICS?** ........................................................... 74

**CHAPTER 14: GOING FROM A DESCRIPTIVE ANALYSIS TO A PREDICTIVE ANALYSIS** ............................................................ 81

**CONCLUSION** ............................................................................. 89

# Introduction

The following chapters will discuss everything that you need to know to get started as a beginner in data science.

Data science is a new industry that is gaining popularity because of the valuable resources and information that it provides to companies and businesses. They can use the information in the findings of data scientists to help make important decisions that will reduce risks, make profits, avoid issues in the future, and serve customers better.

This guidebook will go through the basics of data science. It will discuss what data science is, how to get started with it, and some of the algorithms that you can learn to use to get the information. It will also talk about data mining text and the special challenges this presents to data scientists, and even how to present the information so that it makes sense to those who would use it to make major business decisions.

When you are ready to get started with data science, read this book and see how you can do it too!

# Chapter 1: What is Data Science?

Many businesses already know that there is extraordinary potential for the data that they hold onto. They already have this data from their customers and other sources; they just need to be able to harness it and learn how to use it properly. Many of these companies do not know how to harness this material, and they may not have the soft skill or the technical requirements to do data science, which is why this has become a field of work in high demand. For those who already know how to do this kind of thing, you can really become a valuable asset for a business. However, let's take a look at some of the basics of data science first to determine how to get started with this and what it all means.

**What is data science?**

Data science is a field that helps the user understand events or gain useful information simply by going through data and analyzing it. The results of the analysis are then going to be used to create a decision. This decision is often made by a company to help them better serve their customers, make a newer and better product, and more. These kinds of decisions are also known as data-driven decisions, and they are used to improve decision-making skills, mainly in business, which is the end goal of data science.

At first glance, it is easy to think that data science is the same as statistics. However, when we talk about statistics, we are just talking about one type of data science. Data science will work with a variety of fields, such as computer science, information science, mathematics, and statistics, to generate information from a set of data that can aid the user to make important decisions.

**Data-driven decision making**

The main idea of data science is to work on data-driven decision making. Data-driven decision making is the discipline of creating decisions that have the backing of analyzed data that has been collected from some relevant sources. Without this kind of data, it is easy to base your decisions on experience, intuition, or on what others tell you are the right decisions. However, all of these can be wrong, even though there is a chance that they would be like.

With data-driven decision making, it is easier to make smart decisions and then back it up with proof. Sometimes it can be combined with knowledge, intuition, and experience to come up with the best decisions. For example, someone who has worked in the industry for a long time would be able to use the information they get from data science along with their intuition and experience to make the best decisions.

Of course, there are not really set rules when it comes to the process of data-driven decision making. Many organizations use it to a varying degree based on what they are looking for. Some companies choose to fully rely on this kind of technology, and they will automate it in certain areas of decision making in their organization. One example of this is how Amazon can recommend products based on the purchases that the user has put in their shopping cart.

Other companies would use people to design a personal data collection, using technology to collect this data and then analyze it, and then will use all that information to make decisions based on them. Google does this to determine if managers are making a difference in how well their team is performing.

## Applications of data science

You will find that there are many applications when it comes to using data science for business organizations, public agencies, and nonprofit organizations. Government financial agencies and even some banking corporations use data science to determine a lot of things, such as protecting their bank holders from identity theft and bank fraud and to figure out who may be a possible money launderer. Websites and other online stores will use some automated approaches to create decisions driven by data to customize advertisements to their target customers.

This is not all of course. Social media websites and their applications have started to use facial recognition algorithms to help them make automated tagging features. This is seen in applications like Facebook. Their algorithm can sometimes figure out who is in a picture using these features. On-demand music and video streaming services base their recommendations to the user based on the browsing history of the user.

These are just a few of the examples of the applications of this type of science. Basically, any organization that would like to collect data and then use it to figure out major decisions in the future will find that data science can work for them. Some companies will do the work on their own and add in some of their knowledge and experience about the industry to help them make decisions. Moreover, some may hire out and get a professional data scientist to help them look over the information to provide a report back. Either way, the business is planning on going through the information to figure out how to make good decisions for their company in the near or far away future with the information they get out of the data.

Regardless of the organization or industry, data science can really be used to help improve the efficiency of the whole organization and to improve customer or user experience. This can help managers, and the owners of the company, learn how to make smarter decisions to help them make more money.

## How is data science done?

Since the word "science" is used inside of the name, data science is sometimes seen as a scientific approach to extracting knowledge or other insight from the data. Just like you did with the scientific approach, data science will begin with the use of observation.

In this case, the act of observation will include an analysis of data. This can be done through either an automated or manual means, to bring about patterns from that information. There is also the chance to formulate a hypothesis by verifying the observed patterns as valid, rather than just getting a coincidence of data. Lastly, you will also need to do some testing to verify the created model that you are given.

In addition to being a type of science, data science can be seen as a field of study that is still in its infancy. Because it is still so new, there are some different opinions and positions as to the process of how it should be done. In this book, we will look at three approaches to help you gain a level of understanding and appreciation.

## The benefits and negatives of data science

The first question that a business will have before they get started with data science for their needs is the benefits and the negatives of data science. First, we are going to take a look at some of the benefits to see how it can help the business.

The first benefit is that it can help the business to make some important decisions. In the past, the business had to rely on their experience and knowledge about the market and their industry to figure out whether they were making smart choices. Those who had been in the industry for a long time could be good at this, but they may still miss out on important information that could help them out. Those who are new to the industry could easily make a lot of mistakes.

The data science field helps managers and decision-makers look at information from different sources to help them make better decisions. They may be able to figure out which products to develop, how to provide better customer service, and even if there are new demographics to put their marketing efforts towards.

With the right data science techniques, the information can be combed through in no time at all. This information is often so big that it would take years or more for a person to go through and by then, the information would be out of date. The data science field would be able to help you get through this information in no time so that you can actually use it in real time to help make your business stronger.

However, it is important to realize that you need to look through the data and not always just take it at face value. There is often a lot of great information that is collected with data science, but if you are not careful, you may get the wrong information out of it. You need to take an objective look at the information to see if it makes sense. And then add in what you already know about the industry and the market to see if you can combine those to really propel your business forward.

**Blitzstein and Pfister**

The first step in this data science process is to ask a question that is interesting. During this stage, you will use the information that you know, as well as your curiosity about a subject, your experiences, and any expertise that you have to formulate questions. This can help you direct the way that you analyze the information that you are presented. Some of the questions that you may want to try out during this stage include:

- What is the goal?
- What would you like to do if you had access to all of the data?
- What would you like to estimate or predict?

After you formulate your question, it is time to move on to the second step. This step is when you will get the data. There are several computer processes you can use for this including querying databases, data cleaning, and web scraping. You may have a few more questions that you can ask during this stage to help move it along such as:

- How were the data sampled and will that affect the results that you get?
- Which pieces of data are the most relevant?
- Are there any issues of privacy to consider?

From here, you can move on to the next step which is exploring the data. You will want to start with familiarizing yourself with it, developing different hypotheses regarding the data, and then determining possible patterns as well as anomalies that may show up in the data that you will collect. Some of the questions that you may get for this stage include:

- How can this data be plotted
- Are there any patterns present?
- Are there any anomalies in the data that you have?

Under this method, you would move onto the fourth step. This step is to model the data that you have. You could use a few different options including big data technologies, data validation, machine learning and regression analysis to make this happen.

And then you will move on to the last step. This is where you will communicate with the data through an easily understood manner of presentation either through writing, visualizing, and speaking. Valuable questions to effectively ask to make sure that you can do this include:

- What did we learn?
- Do the results that we are getting make sense?
- Can we tell a story from the results that we get?

**Provost and Fawcett**

With this model, the data science will be presented as an area that is separate from the big data technologies, data procession, and data engineering. It will differentiate itself because it will use those areas to help aid in formulating a decision driven by data that is made across the firm, which is considered by this model as the end goal of data science. It won't consider the other things because these could be used only to improve various processes in the organization, but they are not really there to help aid in the decision-making process.

**O'Neill and Schutt**

Another model that you can use is the O'Neil and Schutt model. With this one, data is collected from various sources in the environment. This could include a platform that the users of interest can interact with, a website, or another type of database. The data that is collected from this source is processed to produce a clean data set, and then it will usually be presented in a data table. This data set will be used for a few things such as statistical modeling and data analysis.

The result of this analysis is then going to produce either a new data set or a new type of data that you would then be able to process for another data set. Both of these are used to complete further statistical modeling. The result here is that they could be a data product that will be sent back to the environment or it is a report that could be used to make decisions in the company.

**Exploratory data analysis**

This approach analyzes data sets to summarize them out into their main characteristics. This may be presented as a visual aid or in some other manner. For the most part, this analysis is used to visualize what the data can present beyond hypothesis testing and formal modeling tasks. In some cases, the results that you get could be used to help with statistical models. We will spend more time covering these in a later chapter.

**Statistical modeling**

Another thing that we need to discuss concerning data science is statistical modeling. This is a model that will approximate a real-world phenomenon, and then it can sometimes predict from that approximation using some simple mathematical equations. Depending on where you decide to apply this kind of modeling, the equation could be shown as a simple linear regression, or it could be as complicated as a multivariate factor analysis.

The equation that is there to explain the phenomenon, depending on the size of the data that you are looking to model, could be obtained through either automated or manual means depending on the what you would use the results for. When it comes to the case of data science, the amount of data that the analysts would use is often going to require them to go with software that can automate the process. There is just too much data present to try and go through it all manually, and it would take too long, and human error would cause something to be missed.

**The difference between exploring and explaining**

When it comes to data science, there are two schools of thoughts that are taking the lead. The first one is a group of those who believe that the use of data science should be there to satisfy the curiosity of the user. They believe that going through the data to find the different phenomena and patterns that are there should be enough for the data scientists and they shouldn't need to do anything else with it.

There is also the second school of thought which believes that this information should be used. It may not be enough just to see the information. This group believes that the patterns and the phenomena that are found in the data should be used by companies and organizations to create decisions. Whether the company decides to do this manually or automatically doesn't matter.

If you are using data science for business, it is likely that you are going to fall in with the second group of thinkers. You will want to use the information and patterns that you collect from your analysis of the data to make decisions for the business. These decisions could be about how to serve your customers better, what products to try out, and what important decisions to make in the future. No matter what, you are using the information to help you make important business decisions.

# Chapter 2: How Big Data Works in Data Science

To get started with data science, you must first understand where the information that you will be using comes from. Data science is not possible without any data present – or else you wouldn't have anything to analyze in the process. Moreover, with the infrastructure that is provided by different technologies – that process a lot of information efficiently – many companies are starting to take advantage of sources like the internet to collect information. This is where Big Data will come in.

Let's take a closer look at Big Data so we can learn how it works in data science.

**The definition of Big Data**

To keep it simple, Big Data are data sets that are too complex or too large to be captured and managed or processed in a bearable time by using tools that are common. Using the relational database management system would not work because there is too much information to process so it would take too long.

Because there was not much software to help keep up with this, and companies still wanted to be able to go through all that information to help make decisions, new database platforms were created. These include such options as Hadoop and NoSQL.

When talking about Big Data, there are five unique data characteristics. The three main ones include:

- *Volume*: This is the amount of data that is produced or received by the company in a day. This would amount to terabytes. Because of this, the volume of the Big Data will be so large that it must be stored on several different servers. This can also present a big challenge because it would take an unreasonable amount of time to analyze the data if it is done manually.
- *Velocity*: The Big Data has to be available as close to real-time as possible. The faster that the right people can get to the data, the better advantage they will have to make good decisions for their business. The information that you collected even an hour ago could end up losing its relevance by the time you can do anything with it.
- *Variety*: Data needs to come from many different formats or sources. You may be able to get Big Data from smartphone GPS data, in-house devices, forums, social network trends, and even comments on social networks. The variety that you get your data from will provide you with a better data set.

**Types of data**

There are three main types of data: structured, unstructured, and semi-structured.

*Structured data* has a predetermined format and length. The pieces of information that come with structured data are ones that can be sorted, grouped, and organized quickly. A good example of this is what you can find when looking at databases like Access and SQL.

*Unstructured data* is the kind that does not have a predetermined format. It is hard for an individual to be efficient when going through the information. They would need software and algorithms to go through the information efficiently. Some examples of this would include documents, emails, social media posts, videos, and photos.

*Semi-structured data* is any data that will not fit into relational databases or data tables, but it still contains some attributes and tags. This type is often called *self-describing data*. This means that the structure will have embedded itself in the data. Examples of this would be JavaScript Object Notation and Extensible Markup Language, which are different data-driven mobile applications.

## The architecture of Big Data

You will find that when working with Big Data, it will come in five layers. Let's look at each layer and see what they will mean for your data:

*Layer 0*

Big Data requires a physical infrastructure that is redundant to handle the enormous requirements to compute it. This infrastructure will be linked by a network to enable the sharing of resources between the computers that hold the information, and it is there to create backups of the information in case there is a computer failure along the way. The performance, availability, scalability, flexibility, and the cost of this infrastructure are all important, and you need to take them into account before starting.

*Layer 1*

There needs to be the right amount of security to make sure that the data inside will stay safe. It is often necessary to use high-grade encryption so that no one can mess with the integrity of the data. Security measures need to also be in place so that you can detect threats to the data, such as a data leak, and data loss should also be taken into account. Access to the data and all the applications surrounding it need to be minimized so that there are fewer risks from human error.

*Layer 2*

The infrastructure needs to employ the storage of all types of data, including the three types that were discussed earlier. There needs to also be some atomicity, consistency, isolation, and the durability of the infrastructure's, or database's, behavior.

*Layer 3*

It is important for the infrastructure to be organized and compiled using technologies that are from a distributed filed system. It also needs things like serialization and coordination services, ETL tools, and workflow services.

*Layer 4*

Finally, the infrastructure should consolidate data gathered from relational and other databases for ease of access for later analysis.

**The benefits of using Big Data**

With all the work that comes with Big Data, you may wonder why someone would want to work with it rather than trying to work with something else? There are actually many great benefits that come with Big Data. To start, Big Data can provide a company or business with valuable data that they can use for risk analysis. Supply managers create demand forecasts and supply planning in anticipation, and mitigate any variance to resource availability.

Big Data is also a good way to help manufacturing businesses improve operational efficiency. When sensors are added for operations analytics at the assembly line, this means that the managers of production can collect data and then create a model that they can use to improve the efficiency of the company – if the information is used properly.

Big Data further helps a business explore better revenue opportunities and whether they are good ideas or not. With a business that is trying to grow, this can be a big deal. They will be able to improve how efficiently they can do research and development so that they will pick out the right products that help them to get the best results with their customers.

Moreover, Big Data helps businesses when they are looking to improve their customer service. When the business has a way to collect consumer feedback, they can create a new database on customer profile and the feedback that they get. They can also use this to adjust their operations and the services that they provide to their customers according to the information that they receive.

**Risks of using Big Data**

While there are a lot of great benefits that come from using Big Data, there are also some risks. Data analysts and engineers who don't conduct the proper design and analysis create inadequate data, with a wrong analysis. This ends up with the wrong data that would be used for decisions in the business. If the information is read the wrong way, it could create a big loss of resources for the business and could result in many other problems.

There is also the risk of Big Data being stolen for nefarious and fraudulent purposes. If this does happen on a large scale for a business, it means that the customers will stop trusting the company and money will be lost as well. This can be hard to regain in the future.

In addition, maintaining the infrastructure for using Big Data could be expensive. Having this kind of data in the company, and trying to use it to improve the operations of the business or increase the revenue, can be two different things. Proper planning and goal setting for this kind of data are important to consider before investing it in the company.

**The context of data**

It is important that while you can get a lot of information out of Big Data, having access to it is not necessarily enough to gain a competitive advantage through data science. Context is just as important, as it gives meaning to what the whole data is about. You need to know what that data means and be able to interpret it properly – or else you are just going to have a bunch of data that is not going to get you ahead of the competition.

Data with the right context can formulate business problems that seek the reasons as to why an event happened compared to only seeking what happened. With the right context, it is easier for the business to understand why things happened. And with the right understanding, a business is better equipped to take advantage of the opportunities that are there for a similar event. It can also take the right actions to correct things if it looks like there may be something harmful to their sales or operations.

Without the context in place for the Big Data, it is hard to figure out what the data means. However, when the company knows what they are looking for, use the context of the industry, and know what is going on with the economy, and the feedback that they are getting from their customers, they find that it is much easier to understand the Big Data that they receive. Furthermore, they can use that information to help them progress into the future.

# Chapter 3: Explorative Data Analysis

With the help of all the available technologies that are out there to help automate data analysis, it is easier to take for granted why there may be a benefit of having the human mind and eye look over the data that you have. A study or research and the results that you get is only as good as the quality of the data used in it.

This means that even with technology, a data scientist needs to investigate the quality of the data that is used. They should not just look at the information that they are presented with and take it at face value. They need to look and see if it is high-quality or if something seems wrong with the process. This is where explorative data analysis can be beneficial.

It is not always a good idea to rely on the information that the other methods are presenting. Sometimes they are great, but it is always best to go through and make sure that the information makes sense. Those who just take the information that they receive, and then run with it to make their decisions, may find it works at some points, but it is not going to be the best bet. In fact, it will often lead to making poor decisions for a business and running it into the ground.

It is much better to take a look at the data. You can use some of the other methods out there that have the technology to help; however, then you need to go through and check the information and make sure that it makes sense before you run with the information.

**What is this explorative data analysis?**

Explorative data analysis, or EDA, is a method of analyzing data sets so that you can summarize them out into their main characteristics. You can use a statistical model to do this, but EDA is there to see what a data set can tell you beyond formal modeling or hypothesis testing. However, it is more concerned with observational data than data from formally design testing. It is not confined to a set of techniques, but a philosophy about how the data analysis should be done.

When you are ready to use EDO, you need to remember that the techniques are used with these goals in mind:

- To help detect mistakes in the data
- To check any assumptions presented with the data
- To help with a preliminary selection of appropriate models
- To assess the relationships and the direction of the different variables.

Make sure that you are not mistaking the EDA with the initial data analysis, which will focus on checking assumptions that are necessary for model fitting and hypothesis testing. It can even handle missing values and adjust the variables – if you need to ensure that you get the right information from the data.

**Types of EDA**

There are a few different types of EDA that you can work on. The one that you will want to choose will depend on the information that you want to use and what you want to do with the data that you have. Some of the types of EDA include:

*Univariate non-graphical EDA*

This is the first step to analyzing the data. With this type, there will be just one variable or characteristic that is being observed, and that is used to help represent the sample. Usually, the objective of univariate non-graphical EDA is to create a better appreciation of the sample distribution and to help carefully conclude the compatible population distribution and sample distribution. Since this is a non-graphical method, the data used for it will be objective and qualitative.

*Univariate graphical EDA*

This focuses on a single variable of a sample distribution. However, when working with univariate graphical EDA, it will deal more with quantitative data rather than qualitative data. Some of the techniques include quantile-normal plots, boxplots, stem and leaf plots, and histograms.

*Multivariate non-graphical EDA*

This illustrates the relationship between at least two variables through cross-tabulation or statistics, like covariance and correlation.

*Multivariate graphical EDA*

This shows some of the relationships between variables; however, like the univariate graphical EDA, the data used is more quantitative. The technique that is used commonly for this is a grouped bar plat.

The type of EDA that you can use depends on the type of information that you are looking at, how much information you are going to work with, and what you would like to do with the information when you are all done. Each of these can work really well as long as you have an idea of what you are looking for out of the data. You can even experiment with the different ones to figure out what will work the best for your needs and what gives the best information.

# Chapter 4: Working with Data Mining

The data that is stored in your databases and other infrastructures has a lot of potentials. However, taking the time to comb through all the data would end up being impractical if people had to go through all of it slowly. This is where the process of data mining comes in. It is a reliable and automated technology that is designed to seek out patterns that may be of interest to the business.

Exploring data could then be the next step after the owner or manager of the business ponder a problem that they think data science could solve – or it could help to provide an observation for a data scientist to look into that could provide valuable insight into improving the business. Data mining can make it easier to help get this done.

Let's take a look at how to get started with this process.

**What is data mining?**

Data mining is a process that is automated and aimed at data exploration. It finds patterns out of a large set of data using well-defined subtasks (which is discussed later). Data mining makes sense of all the large data regarding the absence or presence of the relationships between the variables. It can also look at the explanation of past actions and a prediction to future actions.

The inability to attain a solution to a problem when data mining is not considered is a failure in itself. Data mining is an exploration of data that could create a basis or a prediction for future data sets.

## The tasks of data mining

As mentioned above, data mining has to rely on subtasks to find the patterns that may be present inside a large amount of data. Some of the tasks include the following:

*Classification*

This is the attempt to forecast which class each individual of a population in a large amount of data belongs to. This can help to separate out the information, so it is easier to understand and find the information needed. A good example of this in a business would be "In the existing customers of the company, which ones are most likely to respond to a given offer." This will have two categories: those who would respond and those who would not respond. It is possible to have many different categories based on what is trying to be figured out from the information.

*Regression*

This task attempts to estimate the numerical value of a variable for each part of the data set. The possible variables could include things such as the rate of usage for the service based on the historical usage of each person in the data set.

*Similarity matching*

As the name implies, this task tries to identify individuals in the population that have similar variables to those individuals that are selected out of the population. A good example of this is to find individuals that will match the variables for the customers who are seen as the best option for the company.

The similarity underlies many data science methods and solutions to a problem of the business. If two things, such as a product company, and people, are similar in some ways, they are going to often come with different characteristics as well. Data mining procedures can be based on grouping things by similarity or by allowing the search for the similarity needed.

This was seen with some of the previous chapters – where modeling procedures create boundaries to group instances together when they come with similar values for the target variables. Later in this chapter, we are going to take a look at the similarity in more detail and show how it will be applied to a variety of tasks.

*Clustering*

This task attempts to group individuals of a data set based on the similarities that they have, without putting in any parameters. It is a time to explore, to find out the presence of groups in a set of data, and if there are groups, one can use the variables that create the said groups.

In some of the applications that you work with, you may want to look through to find groups of objects. For example, you could use it to find groups of customers, but not driven by some pre-specified target characteristic. You can use it to find out if your customers form some natural groups or segments among themselves? This could be useful in giving a business a view of the bigger picture, and then you can use this to market properly. It can also help decision-makers to ask some important questions like, *Do we really understand the people who shop with us?*

You can also use it to figure out what the customer needs. Could the business use it to develop some better marketing campaigns, better sales methods, better products, or better customer service by understanding the natural subgroups? This is a concept that will make a big difference to businesses in how they work with their customers. The basic idea with clustering is that you want to find groups of objects – whether they are customers, consumers, or something else – where the objects within groups are similar, but the objects that are found in different groups are not really similar.

You can also find hierarchical clusterings. These are often going to be formed by starting with each node that is part of its own cluster. Then the clusters are merged until there is only one main cluster left. These clusters are merged on a variety of factors, including their similarity or even the distance function that is chosen.

For hierarchical clustering, you need to have some distance function between clusters, considering individual instances to be the smallest clusters. This is often called the *linkage function*. For example, the linkage function could be the Euclidean distance between the closest points in each of the clusters, which could then apply to any two clusters.

*Co-occurrence Grouping*

This task attempts to find connections between entities that occurred in the same transactions. A good example is the recommendation feature of online shopping websites like Amazon. These recommendation features are going to present products that people have already purchased that are similar to what others have gotten.

*Profiling*

This attempts to set behavioral norms to an individual, a group, or a population's actions. It can also look at buying behavior, transaction locations, and service usage. This is often going to be used to detect anomalies in the behavior of a consumer and can be used when you want to look and see if there is an issue with fraud.

**The two methods of data mining**

Data mining through a set of data can be done in two ways: supervised and unsupervised.

When data mining is done in an unsupervised manner, the patterns and the structures will be sought in data that is unlabeled. This is usually used to create the basis for further data mining tasks, which are then going to be done supervised. The result of this is known as labeled data.

You can also use supervised data mining. These are done by going through your set of data with the labeled data as an aid. This labeled data will be used to identify individuals in the set of data. Identification could be based on any variable, such as a group, correlation, or causality. This labeled data could come from the data set that supervised data mining is being done or on a new data set.

# Chapter 5: Data Mining Text

Text is another form of data, and like any other form of data that you want to work with, it can be transformed so that it is easier to analyze. Unfortunately, text works differently because it is an unstructured form of data and this can make it difficult when you want it analyzed by different types of technologies. However, when it comes to text, there is a lot of potential information, so it is hard to pass up on it.

The database of the company alone could hold a lot of information in the form of text. This could come in consumer complaint logs, medical records, product inquiries, and customer records. If this is done the right way, the data that is taken from text could help the business gain an insight into how their customers behave and into the preferences of their customers. Knowing this information would allow the business to create better services, products, and customer service.

A lot of the information that you are going to want from the Internet will come in the form of text. You will find this text on social media, blog posts, review articles, and personal web pages. Being able to get the information out of the text from these sources will make a big difference in how much data you can use.

The reason that text is so difficult to work with is due to the fact it is an unstructured data source that you would normally have in table links, fixed meaning, fields, and tables. It is meant to be understood by a human, but computers do not easily understand it. In addition to lots of different lengths of words, text fields, and even word orders, it is possible that people will write using the wrong spelling and grammar and also with random punctuations and abbreviations.

Because of all these variables, it becomes really hard to data mine the text that you want to use. The good news is that it is possible to take the text that you have and convert it to text.

**How to convert your text into usable data**

A body of text first needs to be changed into a set of data before you can feed it through an algorithm of data mining. This is generally done through the same technology that various search engines are going to use, such as Bing and Google. There are a few different options that you can use:

*Bag of words*

This approach converts text into a structured form. This is usually going to be in the feature-vector form. This treats each document as a simple collection of individual words. It won't look at it all as a whole but at each little part. It will also ignore punctuation, sentence structure, word order, and even grammar. Each individual word inside the document will be treated like a potential keyword that has some importance.

Many businesses like to use this method because it is easy and inexpensive to generate and it will work well for most of the tasks that they want to do with data mining.

*Term frequency*

With this approach, the system will look at how many times a word shows up in a particular document and then will use this to determine how important the term is. The more frequently it appears in the document, the more valuable and important that term is.

Every word in the document will first need to be converted so that it is in lowercase format. This will help because it would count words that are in different cases to be counted as the same thing. Also, words that are stemmed or have suffixes will be removed, so that the system can count the word, no matter what the original form is. And the stop words, or words that are really common, such as 'the', 'and', 'of' and 'on', will be removed, so they don't mess with the results of this test.

*Inverse document frequency*

This approach is used when measuring the frequency of a term in a collection of documents. It is not just responsible for measuring how often a term or a word appears though. It will impose an upper and a lower limit for the term to be considered as important. It is doing this to make sure that a specific term is not too rare or not too common to be included in the results.

Without this option, the data mining system would consider the distribution of words throughout the whole set of documents. This is because a term that may appear in fewer documents can sometimes be more significant in the documents that do contain it.

Here is a formula to use when looking for inverse document frequency:

IDF(t) = 1 + log( Total number of documents / number of documents containing t)

With this, the (t) will be for whatever term is being looked up.

*TFIDF*

Term frequency-inverse document frequency, or TFIDF, is a combination of the two approaches already discussed. It evaluates how important a term or a word is to the document inside a series of documents. The importance of this term will increase the more that it shows up in a document, but this can be offset by the frequency of said term when you look at all the documents. This approach is the one that search engines use when they want to score and rank to figure out if a web page or a document is relevant to a given search query. The formula for TFIDF is:

$TFIDF(t, d) = TF(t, d) \times IDF(t)$

*N-gram sequences*

This approach counts the sequences of adjacent words as terms. An example of this is a sentence like, *The quick brown fox jumps*. When looking for this in a document, it will be considered as one whole term and tokens would be created, so it looks like quick_brown, brown_fox, and fox_jumps. This approach would be useful when the phrases are significant in a document but the words making up the phrases are not that important.

*Named entity extraction*

With the named entity extraction approach, the significant phrases will either be names of a person, a location, expressions of times, organizations, quantities, monetary values, or percentages that will be counted as a term. This would include any of their known iterations when looking through the documents. An example of this would be:

G.O.T. or GOT for *Game of Thrones*.

NY Mets for New York Mets.

These are just a few examples with the abbreviations, and the named entity extraction would ensure finding the right words, even if the user went with a different way to write it out.

This approach is very intensive of the knowledge that it provides. Moreover, it will work well if the person has been trained on a large number of documents or if you hand code it to have the knowledge that you want with all of these different names.

Data mining text can provide a unique challenge when working on mining information that you want. However, since the text can provide a lot of important information to the business about their customers and the products and services that they provide, it is still really valuable to have. You can choose to use one of the methods above to ensure that you get the right information that you need, based on what you are looking for, to make some great business decisions.

# Chapter 6: Basic Machine Learning Algorithms to Know

Algorithms are going to play a big role in all the stages when working on data science. It is used to mine valuable data from any type of data, including the unstructured form of text. It is further even used to organize structured data. And, more importantly, it is there to create and then test models that the business would use to create the solutions needed for various situations.

With the help of machine learning, all of this is done automatically. This is why you should learn some of the algorithms for machine learning if you would like to be able to work with data science.

Going through all of the information on your own is not always going to be the most efficient use of your time. If there is a large amount of data to sort through, it can take up too much time. Or you may end up missing out on things because there is just too much information to go through.

This is where algorithms come in. They are going to do a lot of the work for you to ensure you find the exact kind of information that you need, no matter what it is and no matter how much data you want to go through.

## What are algorithms?

These are complex codes that give instructions. They can do this for helping to complete a task or solve a problem and can be set up to be completely automated or at least partially automated. It is an independent sequence of actions that have been designed to accomplish the purpose needed and, in this case, it is problem-solving. It also has the capability of performing calculations, data processing, and doing automated reasoning tasks.

Basically, the algorithms that we are going to take a look at are there to help give the system the directions that you need to start. You can memorize these algorithms or put them somewhere safe so you can pull them up when you need to use them.

## Linear regression algorithm

This is originally from statistics and is one of the best known and most used algorithms when using machine learning. It will model the relationship between the scalar dependent variable that is denoted as $y$ and one or more independent variable that is denoted as $x$. When we are working with machine learning, this is the one that is used to make sure that the predictive ability of a model is improved because it uses historical data. For the most part, the linear regression will be a supervised algorithm.

## k-Nearest Neighbors

This one can also be denoted with the k-NN. This algorithm stores all the cases needed and classifies the new cases by going with the similarity measure. It will be used to help with both regression and classification predictive problems. A common application used with this would be, *Will a customer pick this product? Would it be good to target them for a certain type of advertising? And is it possible to develop more business with that customer?* All of these are important things to understand how to work with when running a business, and the k-NN algorithm can help out with this.

**k-means**

This is another algorithm that is part of unsupervised learning. It is responsible for finding groups inside of data. The $k$ stands for the number of clusters or groups in the data. The algorithm groups data points based on the features that they share in common. This would net results of either grouping of data points that you can label new data, or as training data.

When doing this in business, this kind of algorithm is used to find groups within employees or customers that have not been given a label. This can sometimes work to a business' advantage because, depending on who is in it, it could present a brand-new demographic that can be used to maximize sales. Sometimes, this new demographic may not have even been considered as an option, and other times it may have been researched to see if a customer base fell into it.

If k-means is used to help with categorizing employees, it could end up providing a demographic group that has specific professional or educational backgrounds, and this could end up being the way a business figures out who is the best candidate for a new team inside of the organization. They would be able to go through their personal team already and figure out who is the best fit for that new team, rather than trying to hire someone new or picking the wrong people because they were not able to sort through the information in the right way.

Using algorithms is one of the best ways to work with the large data sets inside of an organization. A business wants to make sure that they can find the specific things that are needed by the organization to get the best results. Using these specific algorithms can make it easier to find exactly what is needed, no matter how large the data set is.

Now we need to look at an example of how this is done:

- To begin, we first select the number of groups or classes that we want to use. Make sure that you initialize their center points randomly for these groups.
- To help you figure out the number of classes that you want to use, you can take a look at the data that you have and see if distinct groups encompass the majority of the data that you have. The center points are vectors of the same length as each data point vector and are your $X$'s in the graphic above.
- Each of the data points will be classified simply by computing the distance between that point and the center of each group. You would then classify the point to be in the group where it is closest to one of the centers.
- Based on these points that you chose, you can recompute the group center by taking the mean of all the vectors in your group.
- You would then keep repeating these steps for the set amount of iterations that you want. Or you would keep going until the group centers didn't change much between the iterations.
- Sometimes it is best to randomly initialize the centers a few times and then pick out the run that looks like it provided the best results.

You will find that the k-means have the advantage over some of the other options because it is pretty fast. The only thing that you are doing with it is computing the distance between the points and their group centers. It does not have very many computations to work with, so that makes it a bit easier to get the results that you want.

## Mean Shift Clustering

Another option that you can go with is known as mean shift clustering. This is a sliding window-based algorithm that works to find dense areas inside of all your data points. It is also a centroid based algorithm, which just means that the goal of it is to figure out the center points of each class or group and it will work because it can update candidates for the center point to be the mean of the points in your sliding windows.

These particular candidate windows are then filtered during your post-processing stage, so you make sure that you get rid of any duplicates. When you are done, you are going to end up with a final set of center points along with their corresponding groups.

Some of the things that you will need to do to work with the mean shift clustering include:

- To help explain the mean shift, you will need to consider a set of points that are placed in a two-dimensional space. You would begin with a sliding window of a circle that is centered at point C. The point C is one that is randomly chosen, and it will have a radius $r$ as a kernel. Mean shift is a hill climbing algorithm which will involve having you shift the kernel iteratively to a higher density region in each step until you reach convergence.
- At every iteration, this sliding window will shift towards a region that has a higher density. It can this by shifting the center point to the mean of the points that are inside that window.
- The density that is within this sliding window will be proportional to how many points are inside of it. When you do this, you will naturally move towards areas that have more points there.
- You can continue to shift the sliding window by the mean until there isn't a direction or it isn't able to hold onto any more points in your kernel.

- You will repeat the steps above with a lot of sliding windows until you can get all the points inside this window. When you have several windows that overlap, the one that has the most points inside will be the one that is kept.

## Density-based spatial clustering of applications with noise (DBSCAN)

The next type of algorithm that you can work with is known as DBSCAN. This is a clustered algorithm that is based on density. It is similar to what you find with the mean shift, but some advantages come with it. Some of the things that you need to know when working with the DBSCAN include:

- DBSCAN will begin with a starting point that is arbitrary, but which has not been visited. The neighborhood of this point will be extracted using a distance epsilon. This means that all of the points within the epsilon distance will be considered neighborhood points.
- If there are enough points in this neighborhood, then the clustering process will start, and the current data point is known as the first point in your brand-new cluster.
- If there are not enough points, that starting point is labeled as noise. Sometimes it can become a part of another cluster. However, either way, that point will be marked as *visited*.
- For the first point in your new cluster, the points that are within the epsilon distance neighborhood are also going to become a part of that cluster. This procedure will be repeated for all of the new points that were added to the cluster group.
- This process will be repeated until the points are all determined in the cluster. This ensures that all of the points have been visited and labeled as well.
- When you are done with the current cluster, the system will go through and find an unvisited point to start processing. This will keep on happening until all the points are marked, and any that are unattached to a cluster are called noise.

DBSCAN can give you many advantages over some of the other clustering algorithms. First, you do not need to have a specific number of clusters to make it happen. It can also identify the outliers as noise, so they don't just get thrown in and mess up some of the results.

The biggest negative that comes with using DBSCAN is that it won't perform as well as some of the other algorithms when the clusters come in at varying density. This is because the setting of the distance threshold can make it difficult. This drawback will occur data is high-dimensional.

## Expectation-Maximization (EM) Clustering with the help of Gaussian Mixture Models (GMM)

One of the major issues that you are going to run into when using k-means is that it is naïve when it uses mean value for the center of your cluster. This isn't always the best way to do things and can make some mixed results. However, you will find that the Gaussian Mixture Models (GMMs) can give you some more flexibility. With GMMs, we can assume that the data points are Gaussian distributed. This helps because it is less restrictive.

To help you find the parameters of the Gaussian for each cluster, or the mean and standard deviation, you will need to use an algorithm that is known as the Expectation Maximization or EM. To do this, you will need to follow these steps:

- To begin, you will need to select how many clusters you would like and then randomly initialize the distribution parameters of Gaussian for the clusters. You can try to come up with a good estimate of this to help set up the initial parameters just by looking at your data if there isn't too much of it.
- Given the Gaussian distributions that you pick for each cluster, you would then want to compute the probability that each data point belongs to a particular cluster. When a point is close to the center, the more likely it is to be in that cluster.

This makes a lot of sense if you assume that most of the data you are looking for will lie closest to the center of your cluster.

- Based on this probability, you can compute a new set of parameters so that you are getting the maximum probabilities of data points in those clusters.
- You can compute these new parameters with the help of a weighted sum of the positions of the data points. Here you are going to look at where the weights are and the probabilities of the data point belonging to that cluster.
- This would keep on repeating until you get a convergence where the distributions are going to change much more, if at all, from one iteration to another one.

Two main advantages come from using the GMMs. First, these are more flexible when it comes to the covariance of the cluster. This is because of the standard deviation parameter that allows the clusters to take on any type of ellipses shape rather than having to be in a circle.

**Agglomerative Hierarchical Clustering**

When it comes to using algorithms that are hierarchical, they fall into two categories: bottom-up and top-down.

The bottom-up algorithms are the ones that treat each data point as a single cluster but then will start merging pairs of these clusters. It will continue to do this until you end up with one cluster that will hold onto all of the data points.

The hierarchy of clusters will look like a tree. The root of this tree will be the unique cluster that can gather all of the samples until you end up with just one sample.

There are several steps needed for this clustering:

- You are going to start out by taking each data point and treating it like it belongs to its own cluster. So, if you have 1,000 data points in the data set, then you would start out with 1,000 clusters.
- From here, you are going to select a distance metric. This is there to help measure the distance between two clusters. You will use average linkage which will define the distance between two clusters to be the distance average between data points that are in the first cluster against those that are in the second cluster.
- With each iteration that you go through, you will end up combining two clusters into one. The two clusters that end up combining will be selected because they are the ones that have the average linkage that is the smallest. This means that they do not have a very large distance between each other and are very similar. This tells the program that they are similar and need to be combined.
- You will continue repeating the steps above until you reach what is known as the root of the tree. This gives you a result where you have one single cluster that will contain all of the data points. So, with the example above, you will start with 1,000 clusters and then end up with just one when this is all done.
- You can use this to pick out how many clusters you would like to end up with. You would tell the program when you would like it to stop – by saying when it should stop combining the clusters. Thus, instead of letting it go down to one, you would decide on five clusters or whatever number you would like.

Hierarchical clustering does not make it a requirement that you pick out how many clusters you would like to use. You can let it keep going until you end up with just one cluster. However, you can go through and add in more clusters if you would like. This works out great if you are looking to separate out the demographics of who shop with you or if you already know how many of these groups you are going to need from the beginning.

In addition, this kind of algorithm is not going to be sensitive to the choice of the distance metric. They are all going to work equally well, while with the other clustering algorithms, the choice of the distance metric will be pretty important.

You will find that working with a hierarchical algorithm is often a good one to use when you have data that is hierarchical in structure, and you want to be able to recover that same thing. Other algorithms for clustering are not able to do this as well as this method. However, you should know that while there are many advantages to using hierarchical clustering, it is not as efficient as some of the other methods. It takes up more time compared to the other methods – so if you are short on time, this may not be the best one for you.

These are just a few of the different types of algorithms that you can use when it comes to working with data science. You will need to have a good idea of the information that you have, as well as what information you want to learn from the data, to help you figure out what algorithm you should go with.

# Chapter 7: Data Modeling

The next topic is known as data modeling. The data science process is always going to provide you with some kind of model. This model is used to report to the management so that they can use it to make some new business decisions. Or it can be used to predict phenomena that could help save the company some money or maximize the opportunities they have with as little risk as possible. Data modeling can do all of this for a company, and we are going to take a closer look at what it is and how you can test the models.

**What is a model**

A model is a simplified representation of reality created to serve some purpose for the user and which will be based on certain data. The purpose can be several things but is usually there to preserve information that is relevant or to simplify the information even more.

Other than the two things mentioned above, a model can also be used to forecast or predict what will happen in the future, based on the data the company has now, so that the company can make decisions ahead of time to help them increase profits, help customers, provide better products, or at least reduce their risks.

When we are working on data science, these models are there to create a nice picture of the data. It makes the data easier to read so that it is easier to make good decisions from that data. The model is there to provide any explanations that are needed so that the managers can stay on track and avoid big issues. If it is used properly, it will help the business to avoid painful losses that they may have to deal with if they only relied on intuition to make their decisions.

**Examples of models**

There are a few different types of models that a data scientist can work with to get the results that they want. Some of the options include:

*Descriptive model*

These show some of the real-world events that are going on as well as the relationships between the factors that can cause these events. This model will be used by a business to help them target the right people when they are marketing and advertising. It will be generated by using statistics to help pick out the differences and the similarities between customer groups. It could help provide many insights based on the purchasing behavior, interests, and demographics (among other things) of the target group.

*Linear model*

This has a few different options based on the context and how the business would like to use it. It can sometimes be used for time series and regression models. A linear regression model, for example, is there to show the relationship between at least one independent variable and a scalar dependent variable.

*Predictive model*

This is a formula that is meant to estimate the unknown value of interest. This will come either in a logical statement or a mathematical formula and sometimes it is a combination of the two. These types of models will be created and then tested based on some historical data. A good example is a credit scoring estimate which would use your credit history to predict how likely it is that you would default on a future loan. Or an email service that filters out spam by receiving information from other users on what was reported as spam.

*Probabilistic model*

This incorporates random variables and probability distributions. The variable that you use here will represent any potential outcomes that can happen for an uncertain event. This will incorporate uncertainty right in the model and can help the business to look over things that are uncertain for them.

*Classification model*

This designates items in a collection to certain categories or classes that you can specify. It will aim to forecast the target class for items in the data with various properties of an item that is present in the data set. An example is to classify a loan applicant as either low, medium, or high credit risk. Alternatively, with your business, it could be used to classify a customer as an infrequent, frequent, or loyal customer for your company.

**Model evaluation techniques**

Now that we have looked at some of the most common models that you can use with data science, you will want to learn how to test them. You will test the models before you deploy them into the system or report them back to the management team. This will ensure that it will be applicable even outside of the data set which it was built upon. Some of the different model evaluation techniques that you can use for this include:

- *Confidence interval*: This tests how reliable the statistical estimate is. When the test resulted in a wide confidence interval, this means that the model you are testing will be a poor one or that the data that was used was pretty noisy and messed with the data.
- *Confusion matrix*: This tests the validity of your clustering algorithms. The higher the concentration of observations found in the diagonal of the confusion matrix, the more accuracy there is in that clustering algorithm.
- *Gain and lift chart*: This measures how effective a predictive model is. The effectiveness will be calculated as a ratio between the results that were obtained with the model and the results that were obtained without the model.
- *Kolmogorov-Smirnov chart*: This compares how close two different distributions are to one another. Out of these two distributions, one of them will be a theoretical model of these observations. The other one will be the non-parametric distribution that was computed from your observations.
- *Chi-square*: This is similar to the test above, but is considered a parametric test.
- *ROC curve*: This is a shorter version of what is known as the *receiver operating characteristic curve*. It is a plot on a graph that will test how probable it is that a false alarm will occur with your probability detection.
- *Gini coefficient*: This measures statistical dispersion. It was originally intended to be used to see the inequality of the wealth distribution of a nation's residents.
- *Cross-validation*: This method assesses the performance of the model in the future. It can sometimes be used with model selection.
- *Predictive power*: This is a synthetic metric that is used to choose which subset of features in a specific set of data.

- *Root mean square error*: This is often used because it is good at telling you if there is a goodness of fit. It can be used to test whether your model fits the indicators of reality as recorded by your data.

The data modeling is a good way to take the data and put it in a graph or another form that makes it easier to read through and understand. Being able to do this properly and test it can make a big difference in how well your information can be used. If the modeling is done correctly, you can easily use the data as a way to make predictions and new decisions for your business in the future.

# Chapter 8: Data Visualization

Data visualization is important. Even if the data is in a model or a structured format, the data in its basic form can sometimes be hard to make sense of or even turn into a visual representation. Even when it is complicated, the data scientist will at some point need to present their findings over to the management. The management will not need to have the same expertise about the process like a data scientist does, but they do need to be able to understand the information that they are presented with.

It is up to the data scientist to go through and make sure that not only can organize the information that they have from the data, but they can present it in a way that the managers can look over and understand. If the information does not make sense or is hard to read, the managers are going to have a hard time using that information to make good business decisions.

If you are going to make a visual for your boss or manager of a company based on the data that you find, you must make sure that they can read through it properly. If you don't make a good visual, then all the work that you did is worthless. This chapter will take a look at data visualization and what you need to do to get started and make great visuals of the data you find.

## Perception and cognition

Variations in orientation, color, length, and shape are things that the human mind can distinguish between. Even if you have a table that shows the trends in domestic and international sales of your product every month, you would want to consider using color or different shapes to show this information. The managers could look closely at it and probably figure it all out, but you want to make sure that it is as easy as possible for them to read through so you would make these changes.

One way to do this is to have the international sales in red and the domestic sales in blue. This helps the observer to see what is going on with the trends of each in just a few seconds. They would then be able to look on your graph to see when the high and low months are for the sales, whether one is falling behind the other, and if any concerns are coming up.

As a data scientist, it is not enough to just go through and look at the information and understand it yourself. You want to make sure that the view to the manager is easy to understand. This will not only make them appreciate your work a bit more but can ensure that they read through the information properly.

To make sure that you take full advantage of the understanding through the perception of the brain, the data that you present should indicate the nature of the relationship between the different variables. It needs to show the quantities that you want accurately through different types of graphs just by looking at them. Moreover, it should also be designed in a way that an observer can easily compare the different quantities through things like colors or labeling.

You need to use the best visual aid possible based on the data that you have. This will vary based on the information that you were looking through for the manager. And it should make it obvious how people should use any of the information that is on your visual aid. Overall, you want to make sure that any visualization of the data is easily judged based on its accuracy, efficiency, ease, and how the story of the information is delivered.

**Gestalt Principles of Perception**

In business, decisions need to be made as quickly as possible. The decision-makers do not want to spend a ton of time looking through the graph and hoping that they will be able to figure out the information. The reason that they hired a data scientist in the first place is so that they can get through information quickly and easily rather than sifting through it on their own.

A good thing to follow, when you are trying to make graphs and other visuals that are easy to look through, is the *Gestalt Principles of Perception*. This was a result of a study that was done in 1912. It was done to figure out how people perceive organization, form, and pattern. Even today, the results of the study are still accurate.

You will be able to use the basic principles from this idea to make it easier to visualize data from data science. The principles that you need to follow include:

- *Proximity*: Items that you put close together will be seen as one group. If you do not want them to be from the same group, then they need to be spaced apart.
- *Similarity*: Items that are the same shape or color will be seen as one group.
- *Enclosure*: Items that are inside of an illustration and bordered by a line or shape will be one group.
- *Closure*: Any open images or shapes can be seen as complete or regular, and that is how many people will see them.
- *Continuity*: Shapes or items that are brought into line with one another will be seen as one group.
- *Connection*: Items that are interconnected are seen as one group. Be careful how you arrange them to make sure you are grouping the right things.

All of these can be important when you are learning how to group information inside of the graphs that you create. You want to make sure that things that are alike are grouped together, but you also have to make sure that you aren't accidentally grouping things that shouldn't be. When you are creating your graph, take a look at the six principles of perception above and see if you can use them to make your graph more visually appealing to the observer.

**How to use diagrams for visualization**

There are several different types of diagrams that you can use to showcase the information that you are presenting. The one that you use will depend on the information that you are showing and what will make it look the best. Some of the options that you have when it comes to diagrams include:

- *Line graph*: This visualizes the value of your variable over a period of time. This could be over a few days, months, or even years. The *x-axis* of this graph will represent how much time is covered in the graph, and the *y-axis* is responsible for showing off the amount or the value that you need.
- *Bar chart*: This is responsible for comparing values of different dependent variables in the same independent variable. Your dependent variables can be a variety of things, including the income of your company, production, performance, or how your salespeople or others in the business are doing. You can compare them to each other in the same company or even compare to industry averages.
- *Scatter plot*: This is responsible for visualizing the relationship between the variable (*x-axis*) and another variable (*y-axis*) within multiple periods of time. You can also work with a three-dimensional scatter plot to help showcase the information that you have. This one is created when you just add in a new variable on your *z-axis*. This can be very helpful when working in data science because it allows you to have more variables present.

- *Pie chart*: This visualizes the distribution of groups in a population. You could pull information to find out the age of your customers, and the pie chart would tell you what percentage of your customers fall into each age group. This could be done with many demographics for your customers – what products they like, and more – and will provide some valuable information.
- *Histogram*: This assesses the probability of distribution of a variable. This graph can do this by illustrating the frequencies of observation that will occur within a certain range of values.

All of these graphs can be useful when it comes to putting together the information that you need to present after going through all of the data. Often the type of data that you find will determine which of these graphs is the best one for you. Make sure that whatever one you choose is easy to use, makes sense for the data, and will be easy to put together and look nice in your presentation.

# Chapter 9: How to Use Data Science Right

While there is a lot that you can do with data science, you must remember that it is mainly just a tool that you use in business. If you know how to use it properly and you make sure to stay efficient with it, data science can be a great tool that helps limit your risk and even make you more money. However, if you do not use it properly, it could easily cause a lot more harm to your business than it does good.

It is easy to become captivated with all of the possibilities that can come with data science. But if your business can't afford it or if you just try to use it without the right experience or knowledge, then you will end up costing your business a lot of money. The best way to avoid this is to make sure that the data science team and the management team become are aware of some crucial points along the way.

**What management needs to know**

To get as much out of the wealth of data that a business has, and information on the Internet, management must think of the data analytically. If management is not able to do this, then they will become completely dependent on the results from data mining, and they won't think for themselves. There is a ton of information that comes from the data mining process, but you must think it through and combine your knowledge and expertise to get the best results.

Of course, this is not to say that the management needs to be data scientists to understand the information and to use it. It just means that the managers of an organization at least need to know some of the basics to appreciate the different opportunities that it will provide. You do not want to waste the valuable resources that data science can provide simply because you don't understand how it works or what all it can do for you and your company.

As a manager, there are a few things that you should be able to do, even if you are not a data scientist. You should be able to appreciate all the opportunities that this information provides, make sure that your data science team has the resources that it needs to get the job done and be willing to invest your time and money so that data experimentation occurs. Finally, you must be able to work with your team to ensure that they stay on track and help you get information to help move the business forward.

**How data science gives a competitive advantage**

Data science, as long as it is used correctly, can give a business a big competitive edge in their market. To have an advantage over the competition, you must make sure that you are always one to two steps ahead of them. This can be done through a willingness and the act of investing in new data assets and also the development of new capabilities and techniques. It also requires that you not only treat the investment and the results from this as an asset, but you must also treat your data science team and the field of data science in the same way.

With the best data science team, you will be able to gain the useful insights that you need to help move your business into the future. There are so many businesses that will just rely on experience and knowledge to help them. And if you have been in the industry for a long time, you will probably do well. Most of those who are new to an industry will end up failing with this though.

However, even if you are doing well, data science could provide you with some useful information and open up new doors that you may not have thought about in the past.

# Chapter 10: Tips for Data Science

Getting started in data science is a great idea when you want to make improvements in your business, but you want to make sure that you are making decisions that will be smart – rather than just taking leaps and not knowing what you are doing. Having some tips to make it easier, can make a big difference in the results that you see.

Let's take a look at some of the best tips that you can use when you get started with data science.

**Understand the business before starting to solve any problems**

While the data scientist may be excited to get started, you have to understand what you are looking for before you can do the work. Otherwise, you may use the wrong method or algorithm, or you are going to just end up with a lot of information that looks like a mess. It is best to understand the business before you take up the project. If you already work for that company and you do this in-house, then it shouldn't be an issue.

Some of the things that you should explore about the business to help you out include:

> • *Customer level information*: You need to have some ideas about the customers the company has. This could be a month on month customer attrition, a number of active customers, and more.
>
> • *Business strategies*: This would be a look at the way that the company gets new customers and how they work to keep their valuable customers.
>
> • *Product information*: You also need to have some information on the product or services that the company offers. You can ask how the customer will interact with the products and how they earn money through the product. Learn as much about the product as possible before starting.

If you can go through and answer these questions, then you have a good start to working on the project.

**Figure out the right evaluation method you should use**

This is not meant to be a difficult puzzle to solve for you as an analyst, but this is also a trap that some will find themselves in.

Let's say that you are doing the data science to come up with a targeting model for a new marketing campaign. You need to know which model you are going to use to get the right information out of your data set.

The best way to figure this out is to take a look at the information that you have and figure out which method would be the best for you. Some types of data are going to lend themselves better to one method over another, and you will see this pretty quickly. Other times, you may have to try a few of the methods to see which one gives you the best results, or at least the results that look the least confusing.

**Break out of the industry silos to get alternate solutions**

Analytics is being used in almost all business industries. So instead of staying in traditional approaches, that are found with your particular business, why not go beyond that and see if other industries have found the solution that you are looking for.

A good example of this is a recommended video solution that was implemented in the e-commerce industry and can be used when you are doing a blogging portal. However, the only way that you are going to get this done is to interact with those who are working in the other industry. This can help you to learn how to make it happen and learn from them.

If you just sit there in your own industry and try to get things done, you may see some success, but you are missing out on some great opportunities. Our world is changing quickly, and many industries are using the same technology in different ways. Learning how some of these industries use data science can end up helping your own business, even if they are not really related.

**Engage with your business counterparts**

You should not be doing the whole analysis on your own. This will make you miss out on many important things. You must interact with other business partners and discuss what they are looking for, some of the important things about their business, and so on. As you go through the process, you should make sure that you keep in touch with them.

Sometimes this is hard. When you do the analysis for a business, they often want to stay away from the technical details because they are worried that these details would be too complicated. They would be just happy to receive the results at the end and then go through them and make decisions. However, if you want to do the best analysis possible, you must have a constant stream of interaction between you and the people you do the work for. This helps you to stay on track through it, find the right information, and even find some patterns that you may miss out on if you do the whole project on your own.

**Keep the language simple**

You do not need to dumb down the information so that it is watered out, but some statisticians like to use complex formulations that those people outside of the field cannot understand. Moreover, this is even easier to do when you work with data science. However, what you need to do is look at the output of variables that you have and then try to find a simple way to help the business understand what you are presenting to them.

Let's take a look at how this can work:

You are looking through the data that you have to find out which agents would be the top performers once they got onboard the team. You may come up with the right stratified population and the way that you expect them to perform based on the data. In the process, you had to go through and choose a lever which may have changed the population mix. What you would do here is simple. You would just need to implement a differential fee strategy so that you could change the application mix and then this would change the population mix.

During this process, you would also want to make sure that you learn the business language when you are presenting your findings to business leaders. The project may be easy, but sometimes you may have trouble selling it back to a business. And often the reason for this is because of the gap in understanding the internal discussions with the business.

It is really important for you to speak the language of your audience. It is possible to have times when the smartest models are rejected, and the simple models are the ones that the company likes. The only reason for this is because the analyst can speak business to the company while presenting their models.

**Follow up on the chosen implementation plan**

So, after you have gone through and talked to a business about the model you want to use for this process, there is still more work to be done. You need to set up some monthly (or more often if needed) follow-ups with the business to help understand how the project was implemented and that it is being used in the right manner.

You want to make sure that the business is on board with what you are doing and that they are being presented with the most up-to-date information possible. They will not want to receive the information just once and then call that good forever. The world of business is changing so fast that information they find valuable today may not count in a few weeks or months. A constant flow of new data will come in, and setting up meetings with the business and those in charge on a regular basis will make it easier to ensure that they get the best and newest information to make important business decisions.

**Read about the industry**

The industry is always changing and growing. While something may have been difficult to do in the past, in a few months, it may be really easy because a new technique has developed. You can learn from others in the field and even rely on some of the other industries which use this science to provide you with the solutions that you need.

As you get started with the industry of data science, make sure that you read as much as possible to help you out. You can look at books, look online, look at magazines, and more. The more information that you can learn about the industry, the better you can be at providing data science services to your clients. Never stop learning. This industry will change a lot in the near future and having a lot of knowledge readily available, and ensuring that you keep up-to-date, can be really valuable when you are first getting started. You never know what you can learn along the way that could help make your job a whole lot easier.

**Find new ways to improve**

The field of data science is growing by leaps and bounds. It is a relatively new field, but it is really helping many businesses to grow and do well. The only issue is that since it is so new, it is growing so quickly and you will find that many new techniques and even new methods are going to come out in the future. These can really improve what you can do in data science, but it means that you will always need to update your skills along the way.

If you are working on a project and find that none of your techniques from the past seem to be just right, then you may want to consider doing some research. There are always new ways that you can try out, and it is certain that more will be introduced in the near future. Never stop learning about the industry and what it has to offer and continue to learn more of the techniques along the way. This will ensure that you are providing your clients with the best information possible and it can even make your work so much easier.

**Do not make the decisions for the company**

Unless you are one of the managers in the company who has started doing data science, you do not get to make decisions for the company, and you do not get to push what ideas you think would be the best. Your job is to provide information for the company efficiently and quickly. You will, of course, write a report on the information that you find, and in a way that those in charge of decision-making can read through and see what the best course of action is. But you must only write down what is actually there, without any swaying or changing of the information and without giving your opinion.

The company that hires you is not there to hear your opinion about the market or about what they should do next. They can get opinions all over the place if they want. They want you to go through a large amount of data and information to help them figure out what steps they should take to better their business in the future. If you can do this with a data set and present it in a clear manner, you will do well with the business.

Getting started in data science can be a rewarding and exciting career choice. Many companies are starting to see the value of hiring individuals, or at least training ones in their own company, who can go through all this information to help them make informed decisions.

Moreover, when these companies find someone who can give them accurate information, they can combine it with their own experience and knowledge about the industry to help move their company into the future.

# Chapter 11: Working on a Descriptive Analysis

Descriptive analysis is the most common type of analysis that is used in many businesses. This type of analysis is going to be called business intelligence because it provides the knowledge that you need to make predictions about the future. This analysis will include the company analyzing data from the past, using data mining techniques and data aggregation, to help determine what has happened so far. Once the company has all this information, they are able to use it to figure out and make predictions about what will happen in the future.

Descriptive analysis basically describes the events that happened in the past for the company. With the help of data mining and the ability to process the data, we can turn this data into numbers and facts that humans are able to understand, allowing the company to use this data any time that they need to plan out future endeavors.

Descriptive analytics can also allow us to learn from events that happened in the past. This data can come from a day ago, a year ago, or back from when the company first got started. The company will need to go through the information and use it to make plans that could influence how they do in the future.

For example, if a company is aware of the average number of product sales that each employee made every month over the past three years, and they are able to see if there were trends of falling or rising numbers, you are able to anticipate trends that are could influence sales in the future. It can also help a company see when the numbers seem to be going down. The company can then use this information to modify strategies to boost their sales.

Most of the statistics that a business is going to use on an everyday basis will fall into descriptive analysis. What statisticians will do is collect the descriptive data that they can from the past, and then convert all that information into a language that management and employees are able to understand.

Using this type of analysis allows a business to see things, such as how much they spend on certain expenses each month, how much of the product sales percentage goes to expenses, and how much they are able to make it clear profit. All of these could help the business know how to perform in the future so they could make more profits.

**How can a company use a Descriptive Analysis?**

Descriptive statisticians will be able to turn the data that they have into an understandable output. So, they could take a report and turn it into a chart that can show the trends of a company or what has happened to the company in the past. These charts would be used to help your company to anticipate what is going to happen in the future. Other data include those pertaining to a particular market, the overall international market, or consumer spending power and more.

A good example of this kind of analysis can be a table of average salaries in the United States during a specified year. A table like this one can be used by a variety of businesses for many different purposes. This example will allow you to get some deep insight into the society in America and the spending power of each individual. It even has a lot of possible implications.

For instance, from this table, you would be able to easily tell that dentists can earn three times as much compared to police offices; and someone who is looking to run in a political campaign could use this information to help them figure out more about their target audience.

Or, if there is a business that is just starting out, they may be able to use this kind of table to help them make some decisions about their business plan. They can learn how much purchasing power their target audience has and learn more about their own customer before making a product. Of course, this is just one example of using data analysis. Often, these are done to help you to better understand the data that you have in front of you.

**Values that show up in descriptive analysis**

There are two ways that you are able to describe data, and these are going to be measured about the central tendency and measures of variability or dispersion. When we are looking at measuring a central tendency, we mean that we want to measure the data and then find out the mean value or the average is from the given set of data. This means it is going to be determined when you sum up all the data and then divide it by how many data units you have. This gives you an average value that you can use based on your needs.

Another unit that you can use to measure the central tendency (and this one is often seen as more useful) is the median. Unlike working with the mean, the median is going to take into consideration just the middle value that shows up in your set of data.

For instance, if you have a string of nine numbers, then the fifth number would be the median. You will want to make sure that you arrange out the numbers from lowest to highest. This way, the median becomes the most reliable, even more than the mean, because it's possible that there could be outliers on one end or the other of your spectrum and this would bend the mean the wrong way. If there are any outliers, then the median is going to be more useful.

You can also measure out the dispersion or the variability. Doing this allows you to see how to spread out your data is from the mean. The values that are used to measure this dispersion includes standard deviation, variance, and range.

The range is often the easiest and simplest method of dispersion. You can calculate the range by subtracting the smallest number from the highest. This value is one that can be really sensitive to any outliers because you could have really big or really small numbers at the end of the spectrum of the data.

You can also work with the variance. This is the measure of deviation that will tell you the average distance of data set from the mean. The variance is usually going to be used to calculate your standard deviation, so it often doesn't have much of a purpose on its own.

Variance can be calculated by the mean, and then you would subtract the mean from each value of data that you wave. Then you would square each of these values to make sure that you get positive values before finding the sum of the squares. Once you have all these numbers, you are able to divide it by the total number of data points that are inside your set to come up with the calculated variance.

Standard deviations are one of the most popular methods that you can use for dispersion because it is going to provide you with information about the average distance of a set of data from the mean. Both the standard deviation and the variance will have high instances where your data is spread out highly. You will be able to find your standard deviation by calculating the variance and then figuring out what its square root is. The standard deviation is going to be the number in the same unit as your original data, which can sometimes make it easier to interpret compared to the variance.

All of these values can be used by a business to calculate the central tendency and the dispersion of data can be employed to make various inferences. In the long run, these are going to help the business make predictions in the future.

**Inferential statistics**

And finally, we need to take a look at the topic of inferential statistics. This is a part of your analysis that will allow you to make some inferences based on the data that you were able to collect from the descriptive analysis. These inferences can be applied by the business to the general population or to any general group that would be larger than the study group you plan to use.

For instance, if you were working on a study that was meant to calculate the levels of stress in high-pressure situations among teenagers, you could use any of the data that you get from this study to help you anticipate the general levels of stress among other teenagers, even those who were not a part of the study, if the teenagers were in similar situations. Further inferences could be made as well. You may infer different possible levels of stress in some other age groups by using some data that you get from other studies.

# Chapter 12: Working with Predictive Analytics in Data Science

Now that we have seen how data and data analysis are crucial for the effective functioning of your business, it is time to look at another part of data mining that is going to play a huge role when it comes to how much your business can grow. We are going to spend some time in this chapter looking at predictive analytics so that you can understand the things it can do to help you be effective and more profitable as a business.

To put things simply, predictive analytics is just the process of obtaining information from the data that you collected and then using that information to make predictions for patterns and trends in your business. With predictive analysis, you are able to predict some unknown factors, not just factors that come up in the future, but also ones in the past and present.

There are many times when you will need to make some predictions about your business. You can't always know what is going to happen at a given time in your business, no matter how hard you try. But when you use the data that you have and follow some of the trends that show up there, you can easily start to notice some things that can then help you to make some great predictions to follow for the future.

For example, predictive analysis can be used to help you identify the suspects in a crime that has already been committed. Some banks and financial institutes would use this to detect fraud as it is being committed.

**What are the different types of predictive analytics?**

Predictive analytics can be referred to as predictive modeling in some cases. To keep it simple, this is going to be the process of pairing data with predictive models and then arriving at a conclusion to help you out. There are three main models of predictive analytics that you can work with to make this happen including:

*Predictive models*

These models are going to show the relationship between a specific performance of your element in a sample and a few known attributes that come out of the sample. You would use this model with the aim of assessing the likelihood that a similar element from a different sample may at some point exhibit the same performance.

This type of model is often used in the world of marketing. Marketing companies and professionals will use these predictive models to identify some patterns that are subtle, which they can then use to identify the preferences of their customers.

In addition, these models are also capable of performing calculations as and when a transaction is occurring. For example, these models can sometimes evaluate the opportunity or any risk that could occur with a certain transaction for a given customer. In the process, this can help the customer decide whether it is a good idea to enter into this transactions. Considering the advancements in how fast computing can occur, individual agent modeling systems are designed to help simulate how humans will react to various scenarios, which allows a lot of companies when making decisions for the future.

*Descriptive models*

Descriptive models are going to be used to help you ascertain relationships that are there in the data that you want to be collected. This is pretty similar to how a company would classify and group its customers or its products into certain categories. While the predictive models are going to focus on just predicting only a single customer behavior, the descriptive models will focus more on seeing what relationship there is between customers and products.

A descriptive model is not going to seek just to rank customers based on any actions or attributes that they have, but they are also going to try to categorize their customers on what products they prefer to use. These models are sometimes used to build up more models, which you can then use to make more predictions to help your business to grow.

*Decision models*

You can also work with decision models. This model is nothing but a system that contains at least one action axiom. This action axiom is an action that will follow the satisfaction of a certain condition. A model of this is going to use the following:

"If <a certain fact> is true, then do <this certain action>."

To keep it simple, your action axiom is going to be used to test out certain conditions. The fulfillment of these conditions is going to necessitate the completion of the action that you must do.

A decision model can be helpful because it will describe the relationship between all the elements that form part of a decision. This could include things like the decision, the data that you know, and the forecast results that you have for the results that you associate with the decision. The point of this model is to predict the results of those decisions, which will often have a lot of variables that are involved in it. Decision models are often used to achieve as much optimization as possible and maximize certain outcomes while minimizing other ones.

Many times a business is going to use these kinds of models to come up with the right set of rules for them. These rules are going to be capable of producing the expected and the desired action for each customer who decides to purchase a product or a service from the business.

**Techniques to Use While Performing a Predictive Analysis**

Now that we have taken some time to learn more about what a predictive analysis is all about, it is time to take a closer look at some of the different techniques that you can use when you want to conduct a predictive analysis. The two categories that you will run into when it comes to these techniques include learning techniques and then regression techniques. Let's take a closer look at both of these below.

**Regression techniques**

These techniques are really important because they are going to form some of the foundations of predictive analysis. They are going to work to establish a mathematical equation, which you can then use as a model to represent the interactions amount the different variables that you want to use. Based on the circumstances that you are in, there are different models that you can be applied for performing predictive analysis. Let us take a look at the details of some of these models, so you know which one to use for your needs.

*Linear regression model*

This is a model that you will want to use when you are assessing the relationship between a dependent variable in your situation and the set of independent variables that go with it. This will often show itself in the form of an equation. The dependent variable will be expressed as a linear function of different parameters. These parameters are nice to work with because you are able to make adjustments in a way that ensures that you are optimizing the measure of the fit.

In many cases, model fitting is going to be needed to minimize the size of your residual. The model fitting needs to be given a good deal of importance to ensure that each variable is distributed randomly in connection with the model predictions.

The objective of using this kind of model is the selection of the parameters. You want to set your own parameters to minimize the sum of the squared residuals. This is known as the ordinary least squares estimation. Once you have the model estimated, the statistical significance of the different coefficients used in the model needs to be checked. This is where you may use t-statistics. This is when you test whether your coefficient is the same or different than zero. The ability of the model to be able to predict the dependent variable depending on the value of the other independent variables involved can be tested using the R statistic.

*Discrete choice models*

There are a lot of instances when you will want to use a linear regression model. Often, it is used in situations where your dependent variable is continuous and in an unbound range. However, there are times when the dependent variable is discrete, or when it is not continuous. Given the assumptions related to the linear regression model do not hold good completely when you are working with discrete variables, you can work with a different model to help you conduct your analytics.

*Logistic regression*

This is a model that you are able to use in any situation where the dependent variable is more categorical. A variable that is categorical is one that has a fixed number of values. For example, if your variable can take on two values at a time, it is known as a binary variable. Categorical variables that have at least two variables, and sometimes more, are going to be known as polytomous variables. One good example of this one is the blood type that you have.

This type of regression is going to be used to determine and then measure any relationship between the variable that is categorical in the equation and the other independent variables associated with the model. This is going to be done by utilizing the logistic function to estimate the probabilities that are there. It is going to be very similar to the linear regression model, but it does have some different assumptions that are associated with it. The major differences that come up between these two models include:

- The linear regression model is going to use what is known as the Gaussian distribution as its conditional distribution. On the other hand, the logistic regression is going to rely on the Bernoulli distribution.
- The predicted values that you end up getting with your logistic regression model are going to be considered probabilities, and they are restricted to the range of 0 to 1. This is because the logistic regression model is going to be able to predict the probability of certain outcomes.

*Probit regression*

Another type of regression that you can work with is known as the probit regression. These models are going to be used in place of working with the logistic regression to come up with models for categorical variables. This is going to be used in several cases, such as working with binary variables, or variables that are categorical and can take on only two values at a time.

This is a popular model to use when talking about economics. This method is going to be used in this field to predict models that use variables that are continuous as well as binary in nature. There are two main reasons why you may want to work with the probit regression method rather than with the logistic regression method and these include:

- The underlying distribution that you are able to get with the probit regression is going to be considered normal.
- If the actual event is a binary proportion and not a binary outcome, then you will find that working with the probit method is going to give you more accuracy.

# Chapter 13: Why Does My Company Need to Work with Predictive Analytics?

Predictive analytics can be really helpful when it comes to your business. It can give you a great deal of insight into the behavior of your customers in the past and then you can use that information to make some great predictions about how customers will behave in the future. Predictive analytics has had an impact on several different fields and applications, and so far, the impact has been really positive. This chapter is going to take a look at some of the key applications that use predictive analytics right now and how it can benefit them.

**Analytical customer relationship management (CRM)**

This is a very popular application that works with predictive analytics. There are different methods of this type of analytics that can be used to look through the data the company has about their customers to then help the company achieve CRM objectives. CRM aims to create a holistic view of the customer for the business, no matter where the information about the customer comes from.

Many times predictive analytics is going to be used in CRM to help with marketing campaigns, customer service, and sales. The different methods that come with a predictive analysis are going to help a company to meet the requirements for a rather large base of customers and ensuring that these customers are satisfied.

There are many different areas where this kind of predictive analytics can be used in CRM. The main ones include:

- Analyzing and then identifying products of the company that has the maximum demand.
- Analyzing and then learning which products of the company that will have I big demand in the future.
- Being able to predict the habits of purchasing for the customers. This is going to help the company to promote several of its other products in different areas.
- Proactively identifying the pain points for your business that may result in losing customers and then stopping those instances.

You will find that CRM is something that can be used throughout the lifecycle of a customer, starting 0from acquisition and leading to relationship growth, retention, and win-back.

### Clinical decision support systems

You will find that this kind of analytics can be used quite a bit in the healthcare field. It is often used to calculate the risk of contracting certain disorders or diseases. It is often used to help determine the risk of a patient for developing health conditions, such as diabetes, asthma, heart disease, and some other chronic diseases.

Predictive analytics can also be used by doctors to help make decisions regarding the patients who were under some sort of medical care at a specific point in time. How does this work? Clinical decision support systems aim at linking observations of a certain patient's health with knowledge about health. This type of relationship is great at aiding clinicians to make the right decisions for the health of the patient.

Some of the other ways that this kind of predictive analysis can help out in the industry of the healthcare world includes:

- It is able to help increase the accuracy of a medical diagnosis.
- It can help support preventative care and public health
- It can give doctors some better solutions that work for their patients.
- It can help hospitals come up with predictions about the costs of insurance products.
- It can help researchers make good prediction models without having to go through thousands or more of patient cases. The models can be more accurate over time as well.
- It can help all pharmaceutical companies develop medicines that are the best for the welfare of patients and the public.
- It can provide patients with better outcomes for their health as long as it is used properly.

These seven points can have huge industry changing practices for this industry. The ability for doctors to predict what a certain medical condition is with great accuracy could end up saving lives and could even cut down on the number of expenses that patients have to pay into the medical world. Malpractice suits would also decrease, which could, in turn, bring down the costs of healthcare. Doctor's would be able to diagnose an illness better, saving patients, as well as insurance companies, thousands of dollars on each individual case.

Imagine how it would feel if you went into the doctor's office and they were able to diagnose your sickness right the very first time. This would end up with a huge domino effect. You would see lower health care costs, people would be able to afford insurance better, doctors would reduce their rates while also worrying less about being used for malpractice. Patients would save money because they wouldn't have to spend money on medicines that weren't going to help their illness. And so much more.

**Collection analysis**

Many industries have to worry about the risk of their customers not making all their payments, or even making their payments on time. This would include many banks and financial institutions. In these cases, a financial institution is going to have no choice but to start engaging in and using the services of a collection team to recover the payments from the customers who are not paying.

To start with this, it is not a big surprise that there are certain customers who will never end up paying for these things, no matter what efforts they get from the collection team. This ends up being just a big waste in the collection efforts for these financial institutions. With that being said, where is predictive analytics going to come into play here? Predictive analytics is going to help the institution to find ways of optimizing their collection efforts. It is able to play a big role in collection activities through the following methods:

- Optimizing the allocation of resources for the sole purpose of these collections
- Formulation of some collection strategies that are more customized.
- Identifying the customers against whom you should take legal action to get the funds back.
- Formulation of the right strategies for collection
- Identification for highly effective collection agencies.

With the help of your predictive analytics, it is going to be so much easier for financial institutions, and other similar companies, to collect their dues in a manner that is more efficient and more effective. This can also reduce some of the costs that these financial institutions pay for these collections.

**Cross-sell**

This is going to be applicable for any type of business that tries to sell more than one product. Most businesses need to have a lot of details about the customers it sells to. When they have a good database of their customers, they can use a predictive analysis to help promote other products that the company sells. Predictive analytics can help you determine the spending capacity of each customer, their behavior, and their usage, which can sometimes make it easier for you to promote the right types of products to these customers. Not only is this ability to increase the potential sales for that business, but it is a great way to build up better relationships with the customer.

**Direct marketing**

For companies that work on a consumer product or provide some customer service, marketing is a very important topic. This is because, in marketing, the team needs to consider not just the pros and cons of their services and their products, but they must also take the time to consider the marketing strategies and the products of their competitors to get through to the customer.

With the help of predictive analysis, this job is going to be so much easier. It will enable you to see some improvements in your strategies that are used in direct marketing in the following ways:

- Helps you to identify your prospective customers.
- Helps you to identify the best combination of product versions that are the most effective.
- Helps you to identify the most effective materials that you can use for marketing.
- Can help you identify the channels for communication that are the most effective.

It is used to help determine the best timing of your strategies for marketing. This ensures that you use these strategies properly and that they are going to reach the biggest audience possible.

It can reduce the cost per purchase. This is calculated by dividing the total cost of marketing that you incur by the number of orders that you make.

Many insurance companies are working with predictive analytics to help develop some good marketing strategies to bring in customers. They will look through many different sources of data to figure out what their potential customers will like. They can look at feedback data, unstructured data, and so much more. All of this is done to ensure that they can come up with a unique profile that works for their potential customer.

Marketing departments of insurance companies and more can use this kind of analysis to help them out. In terms of the insurance company, the marketing department could use this method to figure out whether a customer is likely to cancel their policy or not. They do this by looking at the behavior of a customer and then comparing it to profiles of customers who canceled their insurance policies. Then the profile will be flagged down. The marketing department would be able to try various strategies to try to get the customer to stay.

**Fraud detection**

- Fraud is a big threat that all companies will have to face. A lack of data can make it really difficult for your company to even detect that any fraud is going on. Fraud can follow any of the types below:
- Fraudulent transactions: This can involve any kind of transaction that is fraudulent, including ones that occur online.
- Identity thefts

- False claims for insurance
- Inaccurate credit applications

Of course, the size of your organization is not going to protect it from fraud. Predictive analytics can be used to detect this fraud. It helps them to notice if any outliers are present in the system, or for a particular customer, and then they will look into it to see whether some fraud is occurring and if they need to take actions against it.

# Chapter 14: Going from a Descriptive Analysis to a Predictive Analysis

Having an intelligence department in your business is something that every company would be able to benefit from. People who are able to collect your data and then describe it in a way that most people will understand can be really crucial to your business. Still, this intelligence alone is not always enough because you must be able to understand the data that is being described and then use it to make the right predictions. If you are not able to do this, then you are going to have wasted a lot of time and money in the process.

Descriptive analytics is going to take the time to look at the business on a macro level. It will look at a lot of data to find values that are important and that the business is able to use in their future analysis. This future analysis is going to be known as the predictive analysis, and it is used to build up models on the lowest levels of the business. These new models are going to include things like product reports and customer reports that will help a business make the best decisions to help them grow.

If you look at the answers that you are able to find on these two analyses, you are going to be able to answer the question about what is different between a descriptive and predictive analysis.

The descriptive analysis is going to allow you to take the time to ask questions about the history of your business dealings. These questions could have to do with the value of certain stores, the demographics of your customers, or the sales that one particular product will have.

Questions you may find answers to with this kind of analytics would include something like "What is the yearly salary of our customers? What product was the best selling one last month? How much money do my customers spend on a product in our niche each year? And more. These questions will give you a lot of answers about the past, 0and they will often be based on hindsight. But you can use this information to help you make predictions about the future.

However, on the other hand, you can use predictive analysis to help you get answers about how your business is going to behave in the future. The questions that you would be asking with a type of analysis are going to be a bit more useful than what you are able to get with the descriptive analysis that we talked about above.

Some of the questions that you will ask during your predictive analysis include "What promotions would our customers want to see? What is the best price to have on a product? How likely is it that our customers would purchase this product? These questions are going to provide you with many answers that would aid your business growth while teaching you how to focus your time and energy on the things that are more likely to increase your profits.

The move of going from retrospective predictions to future predictions is very important, and it is the main reason why a predictive analysis is going to be more valuable than what you can get with just using descriptive analysis. You need both of these to work with each other to see the best results. In fact, most companies are going to use a combination of both types of analysis to help them make changes and decisions that will help their customers.

## What is Prescriptive Analytics?

There is one more type of analytics that we need to take a look at. This is a new technical data buzzword, and it is considered the third branch of the big three data branches. Prescriptive analytics is going to use simulation and optimization algorithms to determine the best options for the future. It is meant to help a business answer the question "What should we do?"

Since the prescriptive analytics branch is pretty new, there are a lot of companies who are not using this in their operations, but there are some who have heard about it and are using it to help them guide their inventory to the right supply chains and to optimize their production. Some of the reasons that prescriptive analytics can be great for a company include:

- It is an effective management tool for the end-user
- It can help you learn how to tell the customer what to do so that you can make more profits.
- It can optimize the experience that your customer gets when they use your product or your service.
- It can ensure that you are delivering the right products at the right time
- It can help you to optimize your production so that you are able to reduce wastes and loss of profits.
- It can help you to schedule and then guide your inventory to the right supply chains.

## The future of Prescriptive Analytics

Since this is a new branch of data science, many people wonder how it is going to be used and whether or not it will make it into the future like some of the other branches of data science. In 2014, about 3 percent of those in the business world was working with prescriptive analytics. Some of the predictions about how well prescriptive analytics would work in the future include:

- The cornerstone of this method, known as streaming analytics, would start to become dominant.
- Streaming analytics would be applied to a transaction level logic for real-time events.
- Prescriptive analytics will have a cybersecurity application.
- Prescriptive analytics will become mainstream in lifestyle activities, including home appliances to automated shopping.

Analytical experts are also predicting the next major breakthrough for prescriptive analytics to be that it is likely to go mainstream and then spread across all industries. Back in 2015, it was predicted that this method would increase in relation to consultancy partnering with academics. Whether companies will really adapt to using this method or not is still up in the air, but it has caught on, and many companies are seeing some measure of success with using it.

## Gas and oil industry working with Prescriptive Analytics

We have found that there is a lot of use of the prescriptive analytics in the gas and oil industry to interpret the unstructured and structured data that they receive. It can also work with this analytical model to help maximize fracking. Some of the ways that this industry is able to use this method of analytics include:

- It can use this method to maximize scheduling and production as well as tune the supply chain process.
- It can use this method to maximize the good experience that the customer has.

- It can use this method to locate any non-functioning and functioning oil wells.
- It can use this method to optimize the equipment materials that are needed to efficiently pump oil out of the ground.

It can use this method to help finish all of the tasks above to deliver the right products to the right customers at the right time.

Since most of the data in the world come from unstructured information, such as sounds, images, texts, and videos, there used to not be a lot of information and data that the gas and oil industry could look at. But with the help of prescriptive analytics, the industry was now able to look at hybrid data to get a clearer picture and come up with better solutions for the future. For example, they could now look at the sounds of fracking from their sensors, images from places like mud logs, well logs, and seismic reports, and even texts from drillers and frack pumper's notes. This opens up a lot of opportunities for these industries to really make a difference in their processes, in how they handle demand, and even how they are able to serve their customers.

**How Prescriptive Analytics works in the travel industry**

The travel industry has also jumped on board when it comes to working with prescriptive analytics. When working with this method, it is going to call for many large sets of data. Given this factor, the travel industry is going to see that they can really use this. They will use this kind of analytics to help them filter through complex and multiple phases of travel factors, customer factors, purchases, demand levels, and more. This helps them to maximize pricing and sales along the way. The travel company would then be able to find the best times to make purchases for their customers and save money.

In addition, the prescriptive analytics in the travel industry would be able to segment through potential customers predicated on multiple data sets on how to spend their marketing dollars. There are many different travel businesses out there, and the competition can be fierce. No travel business has a huge budget to reach their customer, and they want to make sure that their dollar gets stretched as far and as efficiently as possible.

When the travel industry uses prescriptive analytics to help them segment out their potential customers, they can better optimize their money and eventually they will be able to attract a larger base of customers. They will then be able to predict what the customer prefers when it comes to traveling locations based on how the customer traveled in the past. This can help the travel business to make advertising and marketing campaigns that are going to appeal the best to targeted age groups.

Other industries who use prescriptive analytics:

There are many other industries who will work with prescriptive analytics to help them improve their costs, optimize their budget, and provide better service to their customers. Some examples of this include:

- Medical and healthcare companies: The Aurora Healthcare Centre was able to improve healthcare and also reduce their rates of re-admission by 10 percent. This helped them to provide a savings of 6 million dollars.

- Pharmaceutical industries: This method can help the industry by reducing drug development and can really reduce the amount of time it takes to get medicine on the market. This could reduce some of the expenses that come with drug research and could really reduce the resources and hours that are spent in the process. Drug simulations would then shorten the time it takes to improve any drugs, and the patients can easily find trials for any new medications.

- Retail: Many retail companies would be able to use this method to help them figure out which products to offer to their customers. They could segment out their audience, just like the travel industries could offer personalized offers to the customers, and so much more.

The measurable impact of using prescriptive analytics has been able to show in the industries above is something that can't be ignored. While it does need a lot of data sets to be successful, which has kind of limited it to the largest corporations to use it right now, it is likely that this is going to become one of the most dominant data systems in the future.

# Conclusion

I hope this book has provided you with all the tools you need to achieve your goals.

The next step is to get started using the new skills that you learned about data science. Data science is a newer field of study that many businesses are quickly learning is important in helping them out. When it is combined with knowledge and experience in a specific industry, it can be one of the best ways to ensure that you make great and profitable business decisions. Going through all the data on your own, especially if it is large, can be a challenge sometimes. But data science shows you the different methods that you can use to get this done quickly and efficiently.

This guidebook has gone over the basics of what you need to know to get started with data science. We looked at what data science is, what it can be used for, some of the different techniques that you can use with it, and even how to work with the algorithms and the data modeling of some of your projects.

Now, you should be well on your way to understanding what data science is and how you can use it in your own business to make great business decisions.

When you are ready to collect and analyze large amounts of data for your company, and use it to learn more about your business and your customers, make sure to refer to this guidebook.

Finally, if you found this book useful in any way, a review on Amazon is always appreciated!

# Check out another book by Herbert Jones

www.ingramcontent.com/pod-product-compliance
Lightning Source LLC
Chambersburg PA
CBHW071411220526
45469CB00004B/1247